Manifestations NOW!

BELIEVE, TRUST &
WALKOUT YOUR DESTINY

7 Inspirational Stories By:

Brianna Abdallahi, Nicole Bryant,
Charlotte Ellis Colbert, Trina Hardy, Jamila Monroe,
Sophia Shamburger & Renee Sunday

Sunday
Publishing
COMPANY

First Edition

Foreword

Greetings Readers,

The Sunday Foundation Inc. is GOD sent!

Through it, God has birthed this life changing book, *Manifestations Now!* In this book you can expect INFORMATION, UNDERSTANDING, CONFIDENCE, ENCOURAGEMENT, REVELATION and KNOWLEDGE that will help guide you through your journey of life!

Manifestations Now! reveals to the reader that regardless of the challenges we often face in life, there is MORE in us than we think or feel. It releases confidence to believe in your God-given purpose.

In this book, the reoccurring theme to all of the life accounts is to believe, trust and walk out your predestined process and journey in life. Everyone has a purpose, calling and reason they are here on Earth. Through perseverance, dreaming, setting goals and pursuing your purpose and destiny comes the heartfelt encouragement for you, the reader, to do just what this title echoes: *Manifestations Now! Believe, Trust & Walk out Your Destiny.*

I LOVE how it conveys to the reader that there is no hole so deep that God can't pull you out.

Manifestations Now! also reminds us to embrace who and what God has CREATED us to be, to the FULLEST, and to NOT allow the deceiver, which is the enemy, to talk us out of it!

Brace and prepare yourself for this amazing work God has released through The Sunday Foundation, Inc. In the end, you will find yourself MOTIVATED to not only embrace and walk into your purpose, but to FULLY LIVE IN IT!

- Evangelist Jekalyn Carr
World Renowned Song Writer, Motivational Speaker and Author
Website: http://myjekalyncarr.net/

BELIEVE, TRUST &
WALKOUT YOUR DESTINY

Scan the QR Code with Your Smart Device to Listen to the Visionary of Manifestations Now - Renee Sunday

http://reneesunday.com/manifestations-now-dr-renee-sunday-message/

Table of Contents

The Ladies

God brought together an anointed group of ladies to write this book. Learn more about each of them in this section. Through their bios you get a rich sense of their personalities, passions and purposes. As such, we have not made them conform to a standard format or length but instead allowed grace for the Holy Spirit to move in what they share with you. Reach out to any or all of the ladies as their stories inspire you in the next section and let them know how God used them to touch you.

"As iron sharpens iron, so one person sharpens another."

~Proverbs 27:17

Charlotte Ellis Colbert

Charlotte Ellis Colbert

Charlotte Ellis Colbert operates a small, successful family franchise: The Colbert Brand. The company is cohesively operated with her oldest son, Dwan Colbert (DJ); her daughter, Taylor Colbert; and her youngest son, Jaden Colbert. Simply put, Charlotte is mother to three dynamic children and she finds herself in constant awe of their strength, balance and many achievements. For Charlotte, God is first, family is second and her continued quest for greatness comes next.

Charlotte was born in Gainesville, FL, and has two wonderful parents, Earnest Ellis Jr. and Gladys Simmons Ellis; a brother, Napoleon;

and a sister, Kim; each of whom she loves greatly. She discovered her gift of and love for singing at an early age. While growing up, Charlotte would sit for hours listening to the songs her mom and aunts would sing. The infamous Simmons Sisters played an intrinsic part in her love for singing.

The favor of God has afforded her opportunities to sing on platforms with gospel greats such as Minister Beverly Crawford, Minister Steve Lawrence, Bishop T.D. Jakes, Karen-Clark Sheard, Dorinda Clark, Tremaine Hawkins and a host of other artists. She is forever humbled by the great opportunities/venues God has allowed her gift to make room for throughout the years. Those opportunities include completing studio over-dubs for a host of artists/projects including Marvin Sapp's *Diary of a Psalmist*, T.D. Jakes and the Potter's House Mass Choir, William Murphy's *Worship Experience* and Richard Smallwood's *Sweet Jesus*.

Charlotte discovered her ability to express herself through writing at a young age. She has written songs, poems and short stories. She has a hunger to reveal to others how to live a successful life in the face of adversity or transition. She is an author who would like her writings to offer authenticity. While currently experiencing a shift in her family dynamic due to divorce, she would like her writings to release words that nurture the wounded, teach people who have experienced a life-altering event how to allow God to heal the heart, and esteem people to prepare for a new future while accepting past experiences as life lessons and following their unique path.

Charlotte received her Bachelor's degree from Tuskegee University, and is currently completing her last two classes for her Master's degree.

Manifestations Now!

Charlotte would like for you to always remember and repeat, "I can because GOD says I can!"

Reach out to Charlotte at:

Email: thecolbertbrand@gmail.com
Facebook: https://www.facebook.com/charlotte.e.colbert

Trina Hardy

Trina Hardy

Trina M. Hardy is a servant of the one and only true living God. She was born again in October 2004, and has been serving and living her life for Christ since then. Having been trained in righteousness and kingdom leadership, Trina has volunteered and worked in many ministries, always helping out where she could and still doing so today. Those who know her know she is real, genuine, and always raw. She does not hold back but instead speaks truth in love, ensuring everyone is able to experience God's love as she does.

Trina Hardy

Trina is a native of Savannah, Georgia, and is an alumnus of Savannah State University, where she earned her BBA degree in Accounting. Thanks to her education and work ethic, she has risen to the role of Accounts Payable Supervisor where she shines her light upon her office and colleagues daily. She is a proud and loving parent of one daughter, Trinity.

Trina currently resides in the metro Atlanta area and is looking for new ways and opportunities to involve herself in the things of God and help make a difference in the lives of others. Currently she serves as a youth leader working with 5th graders. She encourages them to follow God and their dreams while staying focused on the prize ahead. Her desire for each of her youth is to keep God first and pray about everything, no matter how small it seems. She hopes by involving Him in every aspect of their lives they will grow into our country's next leaders and world-changers.

Being fully persuaded of the glorious and imminent second coming of the Lord Jesus, Trina is committed to the ministry of reconciliation with the mission of spreading the Gospel around the world. She desires for all men and women to know that we serve a POWERFUL and MIGHTY God who cares about every detail of our lives.

Reach out to Trina at:
Email: TH_manifestationsnow@yahoo.com
Facebook: https://www.facebook.com/trina.hardy.7

Renee Sunday

Renee Sunday

Renee Sunday, M.D., is the founder and CEO of Sunday Publishing Company, LLC; Sunday Foundation (non-profit Organization); and RS Commerce, P.C. She is known to many as "the Platform Builder". She is a Minister; Media Personality – Host of Good Deeds Radio & TV Shows; Publisher; Recipient of the Audience Choice Award in the 2016 Ms. Corporate America Pageant representing Conyers, GA; Author; Motivational & Purpose Coach; Grief Counselor; Motivational Speaker;

and an Anesthesiologist. She is humble and enjoys being a servant for all people.

As an M.D., Renee has practiced anesthesia for more than 13 years. Her mission is to encourage and empower others to enjoy life and attain their dreams. Furthermore, she enjoys being an instrument in God's plan to render services to others and to show compassion, love and the standard of care. Her mission is to empower others to propel their message to the world.

Renee's passion is to be a catalyst to stimulate others forward toward their destiny. For 14 years, she thought her purpose was providing anesthesia services until she went from 6 figures to 0 figures in 24 hours. When one door closed, several new doors opened. The doors continue to open on a daily basis for her as she opens them for others.

Everyone has purpose. Everyone has a calling. Everyone has reason to be on the earth right now. A lot of people are asking, "Why was I created?" They want to know what their grand purpose is in life. The truth is that many people are not called to one area or one thing. There are many things we enjoy in life.

Can you say you are enjoying life? If you are frustrated with your job, career, where you are right now, *Get Purpose Now with Dr. Renee Sunday* encourages, empowers and educates others to propel their passions to purpose. One step will lead to an abundant supply of opportunities, obtaining dreams and achieving a purposefully driven life.

Reach out to Renee at:
Facebook: https://www.facebook.com/getpurposenow/
Web: http://reneesunday.com/

Jamila Monroe

Jamila Monroe

Prophetess Jamila Monroe is the CEO and Founder of Jamila A. Monroe Ministries (JAM Ministries) and Senior Pastor at Kingdom Covenant Worship Center in Atlanta, GA. The vision of these ministries is to empower generations to grow spiritually and naturally by fully conceptualizing and embracing the saving, healing and delivering power of Jesus Christ. Prophetess Monroe's ministry draws souls to the kingdom of God through teachings, youth gatherings, prophetic conference calls, conferences and community outreach programs.

Prophetess Monroe has been chosen as a willing vessel to serve God and impact the lives of people from all nations. Her most recent kingdom assignment was to launch and execute the Beyond the Rubies Experience. The Beyond the Rubies Experience creates an atmosphere where the Holy Spirit flows and touches the people of God as souls are saved, lives are changed, hearts are mended and chains of bondage are broken.

A native of Brooklyn, NY, Prophetess Monroe currently resides in Atlanta, GA with her children, whom she affectionately refers to as her "Five Heartbeats". Monroe is an advocate for education and her passion is to encourage individuals to seek their greatest potential through counseling and mentoring, as well as motivating individuals to reach their greatest scholastic potential. She earned an Associate's degree in Early Childhood Education at Kingsborough Community College, as well as a Bachelor's degree in General Studies and a Master's degree in Special Education at Wilmington University. She is currently pursuing a Ph.D. in Counseling.

Prophetess Monroe is a worshipper at heart; it is in the presence of God where the greatest transformations take place. She firmly believes that "once your mind is transformed you can think big and then pursue greatness". The most intense worship for her happens when she is seeking God in an isolated setting, where nothing can deter her from hearing the voice of the Lord.

Monroe is God-authorized, anointed and appointed for such a time as this to prophesy, preach, teach and, most importantly, live the Word of God.

Manifestations Now!

"For I know the thoughts that I think toward you,
saith the Lord, thoughts of peace, and not of evil,
to give you an expected end."
~Jeremiah 29:11 (KJV)

Reach out to Jamila at:
Email: jmilbrourne10@gmail.com
Facebook: https://www.facebook.com/Adeeperbeauty

Sophia Shamburger

Sophia Shamburger

Sophia Shamburger is a mighty woman of God and mother of six children ranging from 10 to 28 years of age. Her main dreams and goals are to be a great example for her children and a living example for what God can do when you fully surrender to Him.

She is a member of Mount Pleasant Baptist Church in Twin Oaks, PA, where she serves on Victoria Generation Choir's Contemporary Praise and Worship team, the Greeters Ministry, the Senior Usher Board, the Mother's and Children's Ministry teams, and as a Shakinah Glory praise dancer. It is clear to all who know her that she has a heart to help and serve God's people.

Sophia is best known for her Lady S. Shamburger "Christmas Celebration" to which she invites friends and family every year and works with local shelters and agencies to reach out to those in need. Sophia and the local agencies identify families in need and then every attendee brings a gift for the family they choose. Those families attend the celebration and spend an evening being poured out upon as Sophia's family and friends provides the gifts to them in person. It is a beautiful evening that the community looks forward to attending and testifies to Sophia's heart for others.

Reach out to Sophia at:
Email: sophiashamburger@gmail.com
Facebook:
https://www.facebook.com/profile.php?id=100008565871358

Brianna Abdallahi

Brianna Abdallahi

Brianna Abdallahi is a student at Wilmington University pursuing a degree in Mass Communications. She is President of the Student Ambassadors Club and desires to become a Public Relations professional who will use her voice to impact her community and the nation. She was born in the city of Philadelphia where she grew up going to church with her family.

Her grandfather Jerome Cotton was a pastor and taught her at a young age about God. When he passed away it was hard for the family, but his legacy has continued through her. She always knew God was with her and has continued to feel His presence throughout her life. Brianna has always been active in the community and her church.

As an adult, Brianna has taken many leadership roles in school, in church and in her personal life. She has a genuine heart for ministry and God's people. As she steps into this journey of deeper faith, she will trust in the Lord with everything that she has and will continue to allow God to use her for His Kingdom. She realizes this journey will not happen overnight but will take much faith in God to trust Him for the unseen.

Reach out to Brianna at:
Email: briannaabda1994@gmail.com
FaceBook:
https://www.facebook.com/profile.php?id=100010497348318

Nicole Bryant

Nicole Bryant

In the natural, Nicole is a daughter, sister, godmother, friend, teacher, mentor and motivational speaker. In the spiritual, she is an evangelist, prophetess, and intercessor. She is a licensed New York State task force chaplain. By profession, she holds a double license: one as a cosmetologist and the other as a cosmetologist instructor, where the Lord leads her to minister to transform women back to wholeness on a daily basis.

Nicole is currently involved with numerous intercessor teams on which she prays and speaks the word of God in the USA and internationally. The two she spends the most time with are GIPA and Gods Relentless Warriors, where she does phone ministry, conferences, and clarion calls throughout the year. She serves as Missionary Society Secretary and as an Evangelist and Prophetess in her church. Her mission is to help people understand that prayer changes things and they only need to look up and reach out to God to see their lives change purposefully.

She is truly thankful to God that He chooses to use her in this season because she definitely does not like what she has been through but realizes it's all for her making. From a young age she suffered depression and didn't see tomorrow as another day but instead as a tragic occurrence. Today, she looks back at the hurdles she has overcome that have helped her become this confident, transparent, beautiful woman of God and she is thankful God kept His hand upon her even when she wished for it to end. She now speaks from a position of authority when she ministers to people because she can truly say, "I have been there and it will truly be okay if you surrender and rest in Him."

"And we know that all things work together for good to them that love God, to them who are the called according to his purpose."
~Romans 8:28 (NIV)

Reach out to Nicole at:
Email: NicoleLB07@yahoo.com
FaceBook: https://www.facebook.com/nicole.nhw

Their Stories

Each lady involved in the writing of this book shared a piece she has written that she felt would bless you and show you that God reaches down from His throne to touch our world. Let these stories, poems and teachings encourage you, build you, revive you and change you. Each has a different format and style, so one is sure to stand out to you today. May you be deeply blessed by each one and may one or more speak to you so deeply you can't help but get up out of your chair and praise the Creator who made you who you are today!

"Therefore encourage one another and build each other up,
Just as in fact you are doing."
~1Thessaolnians 5:11 (NIV)

Unlocking the Innate Strength That Lies Within

Charlotte Ellis Colbert

Unlocking the Innate Strength
That Lies Within

Charlotte Ellis Colbert

Oxygen is essential to our body. Without oxygen, the human body dies and our daily life activities are altered. Oxygen is one of the most essential requirements of life. Without oxygen, organisms on Earth would not survive. Be it an organism that is harmful or one that causes substance, oxygen is imperative for that organism to live.

A virus is a small infectious agent that replicates only the inside of the living cells of other organisms. Viruses can infect all types of life forms, including animals, plants, humans and bacteria. When considering the definition of a virus, we must ask ourselves, what kinds of viruses are lying dormant within us? These viruses could be known or could be unknown and invisible to the human eye. If viruses are left untreated, damage to our physical, mental and spiritual being could affect us for life. It is possible that a virus we have neglected within our bodies has now replicated.

A cell is the smallest structural and functional unit of an organism. Each cell in our body has been assigned a specific task. If harmed by a virus, a cell could possibly be left with a deficiency which renders it unable to perform necessary tasks and lacking the necessary oxygen for survival.

Consider this: Have we allowed the virus of betrayal to produce hate in our manifestation cells? If our manifestation cells are in need of repair, we must be honest enough to identify with the viruses that have been harmful to our manifestation cells, causing near death experiences. Every day there are attacks on our destiny. We must make sure that what we allow to enter into our thoughts, the reasoning behind our actions, and our inner health is fed and lines up with the perfect will of God for our lives. We must make a conscious decision to do all that we can to protect our destiny. To do so, there must be a quickening in our call to action, a release of any virus that is harmful and could possibly cause damage to, or make us abort, our manifestation cells. We will not allow that to happen because today is the day that we begin to speak life into our destiny, repair or replace our damaged cells that lie within and birth the possibilities of all that we are designed to be.

Today we will identify with what lies within, consume foods that provide nutrients to our manifestation cells and start to replace cells that have been damaged by a Doubt virus with a Hope virus! We will only consume foods that nurture our cells of possibility. While treating that current Doubt virus by reading the word of God and making those words become a part of our daily routine, we are positioning the Hope virus to replicate, with an elimination date for the Doubt virus in clear sight.

We will move forward with only consuming words of encouragement and surrounding ourselves with people who will whisper words that produce life, growth, perseverance, possibility, love, success, and God. We will nurture our cells of possibility back to health by reading the word of God, praying, and fasting. With these practices, we position the Hope cells to replicate, duplicate, and bring life to our goals, dreams, aspirations, and destiny.

Manifestations Now!

Romans 12:12, NIV
Rejoice in hope, be patient in tribulation, be constant in prayer.

John 5:6, NIV
When Jesus saw him lying there and learned that he had been in this
condition for a long time,
he asked him, "Do you want to get well?"

Having hope supports life and affirms that we will not lose sight until we have reached our purposed destination. As I write to encourage you, I am also encouraging myself. I am going through a divorce, after 18 years of marriage and three children, and refuse to lose hope of the future that God had designed for me. I am currently living in a metamorphose state. My family dynamics are changing but my faith in God still stands. I have a stronger relationship with my Father, God, Jehovah; and I am a firm believer that, "All things are working for my good"!

During this time of separation from my husband, I do not view it as a time to mourn but a time to replenish the damaged cells with the cells that are creating and preparing the birth of something new. I consider the good, the bad and the ugly, but never have I considered questioning God. My relationship with God is much stronger. I am more in keen with my spiritual being and I know that I will continue on this journey of walking in the path that God has for me. Some of you reading this chapter may not be able to relate to separation, divorce or a shift in your family dynamics. That is okay. You may be able to relate in other ways.

Maybe some of you are dealing with unforgiveness, resentment, doubt, stubbornness or the inability to shatter an Anger virus. Whatever your status or situation, I am a true witness to God's healing. With my refusal to let the Anger virus control my life, I did not allow the remnants from feeling betrayed to enter within. I prayed for God to heal my heart and He honored that request. I can honestly attest that God does all things well. I continue to see myself as God sees me. I will continue on this manifestation journey and become all He has designed me to be. I will not allow this temporary circumstance to dictate my destiny.

In releasing my all to God and remaining open and compliant for Him to perform an autopsy of my manifestation cells, cells of hurt have been replaced by cells of joy and cells of sadness have been replaced by cells of happiness. For those of you reading, I implore you to allow God into your life, relinquish control, and freely give up your will in exchange for His.

In 2004, I recall the moment that I stood in the Emergency Room looking bewildered, unsure, terrified, in need of answers and afraid for my son. My son is severely allergic to peanuts and had just encountered his first allergic reaction. Unaware of the danger he was in, I hesitated to give permission for him to be intubated. I can remember saying, "This is all happening too fast! We just got here!" It wasn't until the doctor said, "Mrs. Colbert, every moment you wait to sign this authorization, your son is losing brain cells because the amount of oxygen he needs, he is not getting." I immediately signed the authorization form.

You see, we too may have what I call "oxygen deprivation". When we deprive our inner being of the oxygen needed to birth our destiny by waiting on perfect timing, not addressing issues from the past or denying ourselves the best of us because we refuse to love ourselves, we continue to consciously play Hide and Go Seek with viruses we should locate and kill with antibiotics such as Trust, Faith, Attitude, Expectancy and God.

Jeremiah 17:7-8, NIV
"But blessed is the one who trusts in the Lord,
whose confidence is in him.
They will be like a tree planted by the water
that sends out its roots by the stream.
It does not fear when heat comes;
its leaves are always green.
It has no worries in a year of drought
and never fails to bear fruit."

The way we rid ourselves from a Self-Doubt virus is by taking the Trust antidote. We must trust God without reservation. Just as I trusted the doctor's opinion about my son's health, we have to trust God, even more if we are honest with ourselves. Proverbs 3:5-6 (NIV) tells us to trust God with all our hearts and to lean not on our own understanding. The scripture goes on to tell us to submit to God and he will make all things new (v. 7). Trust in God leaves no room for a viral infection to attack our destiny or abort our dreams. We must know that we belong to God and consider as truth whatever He says we can have, do or become! It is done once He says it.

Oftentimes pain from others and self-inflicted pain cripple us and has possibly left some of us in a hypnotized state. Let's face it: We live in a world that offers cruelty, places judgment and considers following God a thing of the past. We are constantly judging our looks, accomplishments, marriage, family and a host of other things on an approval rating system designed by Godless people and a Godless society.

Resuscitation is needed from time to time. We have to resuscitate our innermost thoughts and feelings with a determination to allow the past to be a lesson for our future. Buried issues of abuse never spoken, shame, guilt, unforgiveness, abandonment, feelings of insufficiency, betrayal, and a host of other ailments have to become the mute cell—the cells that are damaged beyond repair. We must allow our attitude about ourselves and any situation we are challenged with to mirror God's reflection. How He sees us is how we should determine to see ourselves. What God says about us is what we have to say about ourselves. We will no longer participate in a chess game against ourselves by remaining silent to inner matters that have us bound and have affected us negatively. To remain silent is to mute our voice from being able to speak life into our destiny. Silence is the killer that has the capability to damage our manifestation cells beyond repair. What we speak about ourselves, how we view ourselves, whether we love ourselves and what we deem appropriate for our lives should be based upon God's word and His design. To know God's word and direction for our lives, we must study the Bible, have a relationship with God and follow the blueprint designed for us.

There will never be any two blueprints that are identical. God has an authentic destiny for you and an authentic destiny for me. For us to manifest that destiny, we have to believe that He has given us a measure of greatness that is yearning to be exposed to the world. We must release that greatness that lies within. When we do this, not only is God pleased, but we give a glimmer of hope to people whose need for resuscitation is greater than ours.

Someone somewhere is waiting on us. It may be the person who has been abused, who is going through marital discord, who is dealing with abandonment issues, who is struggling with drug addiction, who is homeless or who is suffering from mental illness. Whatever that person may be going through, we have an opportunity to be a light for them by reaching our own destiny and providing for them a glimmer of hope that they too will be okay.

Proverbs 24:14
Know that wisdom is such to your soul;
if you find it, there will be a future, and your hope will not be cut off.

Jeremiah 29:11
For I know the plans I have for you, declares the LORD,
plans for welfare and not for evil, to give you a future and a hope.

Today we offer the viruses that lie within a teaspoon of Faith. Faith is the antibiotic that kills the virus that causes us not to believe what our natural eye can't see. It will also kill all similar viruses. Having an unwavering faith pleases God, divorces worry and leaves worry on Worry Street. Faith and Fear cannot occupy the same space. To worry about a situation that we have released to God means we don't trust in His all-knowing power and plans for our lives.

Resuscitation is needed on this journey. We must locate and destroy any virus that makes us stagnated and unable to perform God's work. It is imperative that we fumigate and destroy buried issues of abuse never spoken of, anger from something that happened to us in childhood, guilt, shame, feeling of insufficiency, betrayal and a host of other ailments. Ridding ourselves from all of the baggage makes the vision towards our destiny clear. Manifestation of our destiny lies ahead because we have chosen to focus on what is before us and not behind us.

It is so easy to put on a mask designed to hide the issues that must be dealt with. God wants us to cast all of our cares on Him. We don't have to sit alone in silence. Removing our masks, yielding to God's way and allowing Him to comfort us through everything means we will no longer be held captive to vain thoughts, negativity, unhealthy habits and lies. He is waiting on us; we are not waiting on Him. We stand together in agreement that today we choose to starve the silent Pride virus. We suffocate pride by removing each and every layer that is masked, until every layer of pride is gone. Seeking God when we rise, during the middle of the day and at night is a good place to start to unmask deceit and hiding behind false identities. We do this by reading and studying God's word. We consult and completely trust Him with our issues.

Ephesians 4:25
Putting away lying, let each one of you speak truth with his neighbor.

Mark 7:22-23
Deeds of coveting and wickedness, as well as deceit, sensuality, envy, slander, pride and foolishness. All these evil things proceed from within and defile the man.

It is time for us to perform mouth-to-mouth resuscitation on our inner being. We must keep performing air compressions until the pulse of life is felt. Pump until our happiness, marriage, finances, destiny and all that we need to manifest is alive and can thrive without the need of an oxygen tank, mouth-to-mouth resuscitations or air compressions. We stand and agree to manifest our call by seeing ourselves happy while we may, at this very moment be experiencing pain. We manifest our wealth by visualizing ourselves out of debt, we manifest our destiny because we have been designed and purposed by God with possibilities that we refuse to abort.

We decide to trust God, obey His word, have faith, see ourselves in our destiny—in God's place designed for us—we continue to manifest all that we are designed to be. This day we affirm together that we will no longer continue to stand as if we are Peeping Toms looking through the window at a life that should be ours, could be ours and will be ours because we will manifest to become all we are uniquely designed to be.

Genesis 18:14
"Is anything too difficult for the LORD? At the appointed time I will return to you, at this time next year, and Sarah will have a son."

Jeremiah 32:17
"Ah Lord GOD! Behold, You have made the heavens and the earth by Your great power and by Your outstretched arm! Nothing is too difficult for You."

Luke 18:27
"But He said, 'The things that are impossible with people are possible with God.'"

Time & Purpose

Trina Hardy

Time & Purpose

Trina Hardy

JOURNEY TO NOWHERE

Have you ever found yourself feeling lost and looking for a sense of direction? Have you ever wondered if you would ever reach your goals or accomplish all of those things you have dreamt about doing for years?

Often times, I have felt stagnant. I felt as if I should have been further along in life than where I was. I have even experienced a false sense of hope thinking that I was finally moving forward just to experience setbacks, face challenges and deal with multiple problems wondering if I would ever rise above them. But what I have come to realize is that all your hustles, struggles and journeys without God are a journey to nowhere regardless of how sweet and fun they may seem or appear. I have walked the road before and have realized it is a total waste of time.

Despite these negative thoughts and feelings, I have good news! I want you to be encouraged and to be of good cheer. I desire for you to know that we are victorious in Christ Jesus and that the manifestations of God are happening right now in our lives.

CREATED FOR A PURPOSE

Sometimes God will allow us to go through something in our lives that may be unpleasant and may even seem unfair. But this is just a growth process that we all have to go through to be prepared to go to that next level in life. If you want to see the manifestations and favor of God in your life, seek God. Find your purpose and allow God to change you from within so that He can work through you. And in God's own timing your dreams will surely come to pass.

Every human being was created for a purpose. We see this when we read Isaiah 14:26, "This is the purpose that is purposed upon the whole earth," (NKJV) meaning the whole earth and its inhabitants exist for respective purposes. That includes you and me. Jeremiah 1:5 says, "Before I formed thee in the belly I knew thee; and before thou camest forth out of the womb I sanctified thee," (NKJV) so you being here on earth is not by chance or by accident. You are not a speck in the dust; you are very important to God and to humanity.

Let us hear the conclusion of the whole matter: Fear God, and keep his commandments: for this is the whole duty of man. For God shall bring every work into judgment, with every secret thing, whether it be good, or whether it be evil. (Ecclesiastes 12:13-14, KJV)

If you can find, understand and live your purpose in life, you will automatically find yourself living God's dream for your life and functioning in His righteousness.

Several years ago, my life seemed to be on the rise. I was a recent college graduate, receiving my B.B.A in Accounting. I gave birth a year later to a beautiful baby girl. Two years after that, I became a newlywed and moved out of my mother's home into a house of my own and started a new job in my field. My family and I would take trips and travel; life couldn't get any better than that. I had it all; so I thought. I had it all except for God; therefore, I really had NOTHING. My mind was so far away from God, I was only focused on what I wanted to do and what I desired to have and I didn't consult God for anything. I learned about God when I was younger, but I really didn't know or have a true relationship with Him. I was living the so-called good life, but I was living a life with no real purpose or meaning. My spouse and I didn't even know our true identities. Needless to say, just as fast as my life seemed to summit, it began to plummet and take a turn for the worst. I was drowning and headed for self-destruction.

My marriage began to fall apart. I remember how my spouse and I were church hopping—we were visiting and attending different churches without a commitment to any of them. We were experiencing problems and issues in our marriage but I was too proud to go and get godly council from anyone because I didn't want people in my business.

Sadly, we would fight like cats and dogs behind closed doors and hide behind a facade of happiness in front of our family and friends. Months later things escalated, the verbal and physical abuse, the lies, the deceit, and all that built up anger I was harboring led to a physical altercation between us, the police were called and I was arrested and charged with simple assault and battery which landed me in jail.

Yes, I was arrested. Thanks be unto God for His everlasting grace and mercy, I was released that same day with very little exposure. I went to court and was given a year of probation and was ordered to complete anger management classes. To make matters worse, in the midst of going through all of that, my husband ended up leaving me. Money was very tight and every bill was due.

My back was up against the wall. I had no one to turn to and I had reached my lowest point in life. I was embarrassed, humiliated, broken-hearted, depressed and lonely. I was ashamed of my life. I didn't want to face reality or be bothered by friends and family. Although I wanted to hide from life, I couldn't because I had a daughter to take care of. She was depending on me for provision and guidance.

THEN I FOUND JESUS

God saved you by His grace when you believed. And you can't take credit for this; it is a gift from God. Salvation is not a reward for the good things we have done, so none of us can boast about it. (Ephesians 2:8-9 NLT)

So in the midst of my troubles, I turned my attention towards God, I knew I needed Him so I began to attend services. One day during church service I confessed the lordship of Jesus Christ and I gave my life to Him and got baptized shortly thereafter. This was the starting point of my new beginning. I was helpless, and then I turned it all over to God and He had mercy on me.

I became a new creation in Christ Jesus. As I studied the word of God, I began to grow spiritually; and the more I learned about Jesus, God our Father and the Holy Spirit, the more I began to change and want to live my life for God. I loved the person that I was becoming.

God had restored me and He had given me a peace that surpasses all understanding just like He promised in His Word (Philippians 4:7). The hurt and the pain had faded away with time, and somehow a way was made and all of my bills were paid. I completed probation and the anger management classes, and the charges against me were dropped. Years later, after receiving confirmations from God, it was evident that there would be no reconciliation so I filed for a divorce.

God had given me the strength to forgive, put the past behind me and move forward. I discovered who I was in Christ. I now knew my identity. I knew God had created me with a purpose and that everything I went through in the past, no matter how painful, it was all in His plan to draw me near to Him (Romans 8:28). Jesus said "You did not choose Me, but I chose you and appointed you that you should go and bear fruit, and that your fruit should remain: that whatever you ask the Father in My name He may give you" (John 15:16, KJV).

I decided to get more involved with God so I joined the women's bible study group and the mass choir. My daughter and I became very active in the church, helping out in different ministries wherever we were needed. And after years of serving in various ministries I became a youth leader. I studied and taught the word of God to the children while working closely under the authority of the Youth Pastor.

It was at this time, that I discovered that I had a deep passion and love for working with the youth, and that God had placed many talents and skills inside of me I never knew I possessed. 2 Timothy 1: 9 says, "who has saved us and called us with a holy calling, not according to our works, but according to His own purpose and grace which was given to us in Christ Jesus before time began" (KJV). Not only was I responsible for teaching the youth but I was the youth praise and worship team leader and I also helped with organizing and planning special events and fundraisers for the youth ministry.

Prior to me becoming a youth and worship leader, I was always a person who was paralyzed and held back by fear for many years. I feared speaking or singing in front of audiences or crowds. I feared not being able to complete a big task, and was intimidated by others because I didn't think I was capable of meeting their standards. But thanks be unto God who gave me supernatural enablement, I can do anything through God's ability in me.

My salvation, passion and activities in the house of God helped me to discover my purpose in life and prepared me for the great tasks ahead. All that God did with and through me were a part of His purpose for my life and were a beautiful time to prepare me for the great task ahead. The purpose is clear to me now; I can see the big picture. I have not yet arrived where God is taking me, but the journey continues to lead me there and help me realize it is close. I can feel it and I am so excited about it. By grace, I am pressing on towards the mark.

MOVING TO ATLANTA

I had a desire to move to another city, but I feared moving away from my family and friends. I also feared flying on airplanes and vowed I would never do it. By not adhering to the reminder in 2 Timothy 1:7 (KJV), I really limited myself and missed out on great opportunities all because I let fear of the unknown set in: "For God hath not give us the spirit of fear; but of power, and of love, and of a sound mind." However, becoming a youth leader challenged me and helped me to overcome some of those fears. I had to sing, speak out and pray in front of people. I had to complete tasks that were assigned to me that seemed way too big for me to do on my own.

I saw the manifestations of God moving and working all around me and through me. To my surprise, I was successful in everything that I was asked and sent out to do. I was amazed because I knew it was God's grace and Him empowering me. There is no way I could have performed and done all of those things on my own without God. Overcoming my fears allowed doors to open and opportunities to come my way that I had not planned.

I had the honor of being a backup singer for an amazing local gospel artist, and on another occasion I was invited to sing with another great recording artist in his women's gospel group. I have truly seen a significant increase in the manifestations of God's favor in my life.

After months of being unemployed, laid off and released from multiple jobs, I decided to search outside of Savannah, GA. In March of 2014, I went to a job interview near Atlanta and within an hour of leaving the interview, I was called with an offer. I said, "Yes," to the job offer and I moved to the metro Atlanta area.

God is always faithful; He ordered my steps. Every step moved me closer to my original purpose for creation. In the process, I miraculously met my fiancé! God has given us similar dreams, passions and purpose in life. Later in December of 2014, I flew on an airplane for the very first time overseas to meet and spend the holidays with my then boyfriend, his family and his friends. On January 1, 2015, during Watch Night service, my then boyfriend of more than three years asked if he could have my hand in marriage. He proposed to me and I said, "Yes"! So today, I am happily engaged. I have been blessed to be connected to a man who loves God just as much as I do. He is not only knowledgeable and passionate about the things of God but he's also walking in his purpose and living his life for Christ.

THE WAIT AND THE TIME

Though we were first introduced in 2012, we couldn't meet until December 2014. Our two years of waiting was more purposeful and productive than many marriages. We waited on God, prayed, fasted, shared the word of God and also completed projects together. He is a major motivation in my life and I am his motivation too. We are setting our focus on Jesus, His glorious coming and global evangelization. Working for God is our big picture.

My fiancé and I are currently embarking on a journey that's going to require tremendous faith and much patience and endurance for us to reach our goals in pursuit of fulfilling what God has purposed us to do as a couple and as a family. This is where many people miss it: doing things God's way may take longer. The purpose is clear but we have to be very careful with the timing. We know it's going to require us to be patient and sensitive to God's timing even when the wait seems as if it's taking forever; but the integrity of the word of God is unquestionable. The Bible says "He has made everything beautiful in its time. He has also set eternity in the human heart; yet no one can fathom what God has done from beginning to end" (Ecclesiastes 3:11, NIV). And "There is a time for everything, and a season for every activity under the heavens" (Ecclesiastes 3:1, NIV).

The fact that you find your purpose in life doesn't mean you will start living your exact purpose. There is always a time of training and preparation. Our Lord Jesus had to wait until He was 30 years old, though

He knew His purpose as a child and walked in the consciousness of His purpose. David served as a servant in the palace in which he was anointed to be a king. The anointing was on him as the king but he served Saul who had already been rejected by God. He was persecuted, maltreated and faced with death many times before he started his purpose in life. That was his waiting time.

In our case, it is not easy living separately but we are learning that to be successful in our purpose for living, we must put God first in our lives and acknowledge Him in all of our ways and He will direct our paths. We have to be careful not to rush into something before its time, or season, or else the result could be failure. If we fail the first time, should we give up? Of course not! We pray, we seek God for guidance, we wait for His answer and we try again if He tells you, "Yes".

We can save ourselves a lot of money, time and energy when we are walking in God's timing and not our own. God has made promises to us in His word. To those of us who have confessed Christ as our Lord and Savior, we are eligible to receive all of the benefits that God has promised us in His Word. We are more than conquerors and we are victorious in Christ Jesus! Therefore, when the time has come, you will automatically find yourself living the purpose of God for your life. God likes to use men and women who are in service or serving others. But before we can be great leaders we must first learn how to be good servants. Make sure you live in faith, in obedience and aligned with what God has called you to be. Be careful not to get caught up in comparing or basing your success on other people's success. And don't allow others to try to shape and model you into what they think you should be. God has made us all unique, and has gifted us with different talents and abilities.

Whatever your talent and skills are, work on perfecting them and be the best YOU that you can be.

OUR WALK OF FAITH

Discovering, understanding and living your purpose in life is a journey of faith. The Bible tells us that, "…without faith it is impossible to please God, because anyone who comes to Him must believe that He exists and that He rewards those who earnestly seek Him." (Hebrews 11:6, NIV). You must raise your faith level. The Christian life is a life of faith and to live the life God purposed for you, you must be aligned with His words, which will automatically boost your faith. And at this point, you will do more than trust Him—you will have enough wisdom to meditate and speak forth the word of God into reality. You will be able to face the challenges of life head on and come out victoriously.

We will still face challenges and setbacks when we know our purpose and are willing to function in it, but if we continue to trust in God, step out on faith, meditate on the word of God and speak the word to our situations, we will overcome the obstacles. God has already sent His Holy Spirit to comfort, lead and empower us. It is in our weaknesses that God's strength is made perfect, but we have to play our roles too by walking in faith, by working hard and by not giving up.

As women, it is important for us to know that we are gifts from God. He created us with a purpose long before we were born. If you want to be successful, and have a thriving business, career, loving spouse or purpose-driven family, PUT GOD FIRST! The Bible says, "But seek first the kingdom of God and His righteousness, and all these things shall be added to you" (Matthew 6:33, NIV). God has equipped us with everything we need to be successful in life.

God is our source. He has made resources available to us to help sharpen our skills and abilities, and to enhance our knowledge. He will also connect us with the right people who will help push us to reach our dreams and purposes in life. When you submit to Him and surrender your life into His hands, you will find that the Holy Spirit will align you with people who will propel you into the future He has planned for you. The first step is surrendering to Him fully.

MY CHALLENGE TO YOU

Fast & Pray: Pray and make your requests known to God. Talk to Him about your dreams, your desires and your plans. Ask Him for guidance. Fast & pray when you have big decisions to make. Don't be in a hurry; wait for God's answer. Be sure to praise God and thank Him in advance for answered prayers.

Plan: Write down your plans and goals. Ensure they are plans that will glorify God and help make a difference in others' lives as well as your own. Remember it's okay to plan, but just know that God may step in and take control and make changes to your plans because He knows what's best.

Invest in the kingdom of God and invest in yourself: Sharpen your skills and be sure to use your God-given talents, gifts and abilities not only for work but also for kingdom building.

Study: Spend some time everyday in God's Word. Find those Bible scriptures that pertain to God's promises. Write them down, mediate on them and speak them over your life.

A Good Place To Be: The Potter's Wheel

Renee Sunday

A Good Place To Be: The Potter's Wheel

Renee Sunday

As a child I would dream about riding on a big carousel with glowing and magical colors or to just ride a merry-go-round every day of my life. I loved the fresh air in my face and the jiggle in my tummy…like Jell-O. I didn't know at the time that I was carefree and on top of the world. Several years after that, I didn't know I was growing up in an environment where people believed deeply the myth that I wasn't going to excel, wouldn't finish high school, would have children at an early age and was not worthy to be in college or own a car, home or business. Who would have thought I was on the Potter's wheel of my Heavenly Father? My parents instilled in me from an early age that I was beautiful, smart and could do anything through God. Throughout life, I have remembered these words when life happens and I feel challenged.

My foundation was in a Christian home. We ate food together, went to church together and played together. I always gleaned from my sister, San, for everything: knowledge, safety and wisdom. I was known as "the tag-along sister" and "the church girl". My classmates would call me "four-eyed" and "skinny" because as long as I remembered I wore glasses and was tall as a corn stalk. I would cry when my classmates called me names and talked about my glasses. Each time I told my parents, they would say, "You are beautiful and smart. Don't listen to them." I did what my parents said. I walked with love, peace and happiness. I soared in school being the Class President and Valedictorian of my high school class, as well as excelled in college and medical school. I knew deep down inside I was going to be an amazing person. I knew I would become an Anesthesiologist, get married by 30, have a house with a white picket fence and would create 2.5 children—just like society said I should.

But that is not how my story unfolded.

I practiced anesthesia for 13 years and lost my job not once but twice. Downsizing was in the air. The second time I went from six figures to zero figure in one day—yes, in 24 hours. I had peace about the situation. I knew inside when God closes one door several others open. When I sat down to think about it, I cried and I was embarrassed. I wondered, "How does a physician lose a job?" I was afraid to tell my family. When I told my parents, they said the same thing they did when I was growing up, "You are smart, beautiful and wonderfully made." They resonated with what was inside of me. We knew God's plan was best and that everything would work out for my good as promised in Romans 8:28.

In the years before I lost my job, my beloved brother William Sunday, Jr. passed away. What a life crisis for my family! Junior was known for his gentleness and love for everyone he met. We were angry, depressed and sad. Every phase of the grief process was expressed within my family. We bonded together for support and to uplift each other. We leaned on God and knew in our hearts that God would equip us with what we needed to move forward in life. William Jr. would have wanted us to pursue our dreams, goals, purposes and destinies in life. So when I lost my job, I knew God would give me direction to move forward from this difficult situation—and He did.

I gained joy through journaling, which helped relieve my pain from my brother's passing and losing my job twice. Journaling allowed me to express my thoughts, dreams and cares in writing. Before I realized what I was truly doing, I had penned a vast amount of gems about life. My journals transformed into a book entitled *Sunday Grief, M.D.*, which helps others throughout the world when difficult situations arise in their lives.

My joy of writing was birthed through a difficult situation. I have heard scholars say, "No Pain ... No Glory," and "You have to go through pain to get to manifestations". I can truly say this was painful, but I can say God is my healer and deliverer when a trial or tribulation occurs.

With the discovery of the internet to market my book, I discovered the pull of posting motivational, inspirational and empowerment posts with a zeal to help others to experience the love, peace, joy and happiness that comes when we accept Him as Savior. As I continued my journey, people started to contact me about how they could be happy and love the Lord. I gleamed at the honor to tell others of His Love.

One day after meditation and prayer, I was asked by a minister, "Have you considered media because you are sooo motivating?" I answered, "No way". I did have a peace inside about it. I jumped at this opportunity to walk into a new territory with God for my direction.

My media debut was a blast. I noticed there was a leap in my belly, in my soul, when the producer said, "Lights, Camera, Action". I continued to gain knowledge, wisdom and joy in media. God blessed me with the opportunity to launch a new radio and TV Show. God gave me the name: Good Deeds. Presently, I glow every time I have the opportunity to help others show their light to the world. I can truly shout from the mountaintop. I'm walking in my Purpose. God created me to help others to believe, trust and walk in their destiny.

My life has evolved and continues to do so—just like the merry-go-round that I dreamed of as a child. I'm on the Potter's wheel. Trials and tribulations will come, but I know God has an amazing plan for me. I have to believe, trust and walk in my destiny by leaning on God not myself.

To the readers of this book, you have a calling, purpose and destiny. There is a reason you were born. You may be searching for your purpose and destiny. All is well. It's a process. You will make mistakes and will have times when you make what you deem as a wrong turn. But God already has a way of escape. God sent His Son, Jesus, just for you that you can have a right to the tree of life.

You may feel discouraged today, wondering what is going on because you have been walking with God, making the right decisions and doing everything you feel He has asked you to do. Don't give up. Instead press in more fully and ask Him what you are holding back that He wants from you. For some of you it will be a job that He has told you to move from, for others it will be forgiveness you need to extend to someone. Others may find that He wants you to return to school so you can enter a new field of opportunity He is preparing for you. And still for others it is going to be giving up the need to control every detail of your life. Search your heart and ask Him what you are withholding that He wants from you and then surrender fully to His will and His way. He will do more in a day than you could do in years. Trust Him and give it all to Him.

On the Potter's wheel, you become like clay, willing to be molded by the God who created the heavens and earth, moon and sun and all that is within this world. You give God the permission to mold you and make you beautiful. To remove the dross and form you into the beautiful woman or man of God He destined you to be. Don't hold back. Release it all today and surrender FULLY to His will.

John 3:16, KJV
For God so loved the world, that he gave his only begotten Son, that whosoever believeth in him should not perish, but have everlasting life.

You will live out your dreams, goals, passion, purpose and destiny. "Trust in the Lord and lean not to your own understanding. In all thy ways acknowledge Him and He will direct your paths" (Proverbs 3:5-6, KJV).

Manifestations Now! Believe, Trust and Walk out Your Destiny in Your Life.

God loves you.

Selah.

Push Past It All. You're Worth It

Jamila Monroe

Push Past It All. You're Worth It

Jamila Monroe

Finding her…who is she? She is me. You might find her in you. Your story may be similar to my story. The hardest part of allowing God to redefine you is that it takes the willingness on your part to revisit the hurtful events from your past. It requires you to go back into every day, month and year of your life and find the cause of the breakdown so you can become the best that God has ordained. It takes complete honesty to figure out what went wrong. Was it your fault or someone else's? Was there something that you could have done better? Perhaps you've lost yourself in your childhood, or maybe in your adulthood, but no matter how lost you may feel God wants you to find yourself in the missing pieces of your trials, tribulations and circumstances. When you find yourself you can return back to the original plan that God put in place before you were in your mother's womb. Not another day will you be lost or confused regarding who you are or what God has called you to be. This is the moment where your life shifts and you find YOU…when you find you will realize what's waiting to be unleashed are big dreams, large visions, abundance of purposes and a person so strong you are unmovable.

Neglect means "to fail to take care of or to give attention to (someone or something); to fail to do (something)" (Miriam Webster, 2016). It was Easter '82 as my sisters and I sat on the couch in disbelief. He had promised one too many times that he was going to come get us; something in me thought this time was different. As each hour passed, our hair began to frizz, our nicely ironed dresses began to be wrinkled and our little bit of hope became crushed. The moment it became dark, I knew he wasn't coming and that this was the day the seed of neglect and rejection was planted. How could someone who was supposed to take care of us, love us, protect us and provide for us cause this type of disappointment? At that very moment I realized if a father can do this to his children, then the presence of anyone within my life was not guaranteed to remain stable. I held on to that belief year after year.

When people entered my life, I would automatically give them an expiration date. I would think, "I wonder how long it's going to take before they leave." This neglect caused me to even enter relationships with no hopes that they would last forever, so before anyone could hurt me I was able to guard myself with a wall. The worst feeling of my dad neglecting me was knowing he was somewhere else taking care of three other children. It's not that he was off chilling single—he had the responsibility of other kids and followed through. So in my mind it had to be something wrong with me.

This day was a pivotal moment in my experience with neglect. Little did I know there would be many more to follow. I didn't realize at the time that me being neglected was actually God's perfection—part of His perfect plan. Our worth is not defined by what family we come from, it is defined by the ultimate sacrifice on the cross. There are many people that come from a dysfunctional family yet are able to function and be successful. Psalms 27:10 tells us that when our fathers and mothers forsake us, the Lord will take us up (NIV). I didn't know at the time that the Lord was there from the beginning, and perhaps was shielding me from something that could hurt me worse.

In the biblical story of Ishmael and Abraham (Genesis 16), Abraham went ahead of the will of God when his wife Sarah asked him to sleep with her maidservant so they could have a child. When the child was born and Sarah began to see the closeness of Abraham and Ishmael, she asked Abraham to kick them out of the house. She wanted him to be done with them. I can only imagine the neglect and rejection that Ishmael felt. His parent's mistake was now fallen on him and he would have to pay year after year. But the good thing about this story is that the Bible states that God made a promise to Abraham, and the Lord ended up taking care of Ishmael and his mother Hagar. It is very unfortunate that Ishmael had to even give up what was rightfully his as the first born son. Though I never understood how parents neglect their children, I soon realized that out of every bad incident something great can come forth.

Rejection is "the act of rejecting," which means "to refuse to believe, accept, or consider (something)" (Miriam Webster, 2016). Rejection can be very painful and hurtful, but it can also be the motivating force that propels you to love more, do more and be more. Rejection is part of life and most of us will have to deal with it at some point. We must be willing to take the negativity and turn it into positivity. Rejection can happen on different levels personally, spiritually, professionally and socially.

In the Bible, the story of Joseph is one of the greatest stories of an individual overcoming the pains of rejection. Joseph was favored by his father so much that He was given a coat of many colors, which made his brothers jealous. Joseph shared with them that he had a dream in which he would actually one day rule over them. It caused them to hate him even more. These feelings magnified to the point that they decided to throw him in a pit. Joseph had endured various trials along the way to the pit, then the prison. I'm sure his brothers thought it was the end of him—

that they had gotten rid of Joseph—but they had actually given him the push he needed to propel him to his palace. Joseph displayed humility upon seeing his brothers again years later. Instead of doing to them what they did to him, he showed them kindness.

Similar to Joseph, I suffered from two forms of rejection: within and from others. I rejected the fact that God made me in His image and likeness. One day I uttered these words, "If I hear another person say how beautiful I am, I'm going to scream". That was my reaction every time I received a compliment. Did they not see the imperfections in my body structure? Did they not see how light-skinned I am? Did they not see my insufficiencies? For years I tried to find something or someone to accept me. Despite the compliments, I saw something completely different in my mirror. I never felt pretty; in fact, when I was finally allowed to wear makeup, I would use it as a cover-up. In my mind there were something more than baggy eyes, pimples, blemishes, freckles that I wanted to hide. Instead of accepting the way God made me, I always found fault in my appearance. There were days when I cried myself to sleep; I wanted to wake up and look different. At times in school I was teased on my looks, to the point of me being confused. I didn't understand why some people complimented me while others went out of their way to reject me. I felt like I didn't fit in anywhere.

Misconception is "a view or opinion that is incorrect because it's based on faulty thinking or understanding" (Google, 2016). Many people allow the opinions of others to define how they live, how they love and how they pursue their dreams. After a while they begin to believe the lies of the enemy. When they believe that they are insignificant and don't belong, they halt their life.

The Israelites were a people who saw God's miracles firsthand. They saw their enemies devoured, they witnessed the miracles of the Red Sea being parted, they saw the Lord provide manna for them, and they were now camped so close to the Promised Land that they should have been celebrating the promises of the Lord. Instead, their misconception of their situation held them back. Numbers 13 tells us that men explored the land of Canaan, which God was giving to the Israelites. The land was overflowing with milk, honey and fruit but the cities were fortified and very large. The men noted that because of the greatness of the land, they felt like grasshoppers within it (NIV). This was the land that the Lord had promised to them, but because of what they saw—what they thought they were faced with—they viewed themselves as grasshoppers. We can truly limit ourselves by our misconceptions and what we think about who we are. We must understand our identity so we don't misunderstand what God is trying to do within us.

In June of 1993, I remember thinking, "This is happening…this might be my "it" thing: the one thing I've been waiting on for self-fulfillment, the one thing that will love me unconditionally, the one person that would love me beyond my faults and would make everything in my life right." I was 17 years old, sitting at the table, and hearing my mom ask me and my three sisters, "Is there anything that either one of you want to tell me"? At that point I knew the cat was out the bag: someone told my mom I was pregnant. As I begin to see the hurt and disappointment in my mom's eyes, I figured this was not the answer to my solution. Every month of my pregnancy I looked forward to the day of delivery, knowing it wasn't going to be easy. I was a proud mother at a young age, but after years went by I understood not even my daughter could fill the place of me loving myself more.

Agitation is "that state of anxiety or nervous excitement; the action of briskly stirring or disturbing something" (Google, 2016). "I hear you Lord, you don't have to disturb my sleep, my peace." I had to go through different circumstances in which I lost things, lost people and lost my will. Every situation enabled me to learn an important aspect of trusting the Lord with all my heart and soul.

On the most disturbing day of my life this far, I was in the middle of a divorce and had just moved from a 3,000 square foot house to a 900 square foot house with nothing but my kids—no furniture, dishes…nothing. I got to a point where I couldn't even provide for them. We didn't have milk, bread or even anything worth cooking. I heard the Lord say, "Will you trust me?" I said, "Yes, Lord, I will trust you". He said, "NO. WILL YOU TRUST ME?" Something prompted me to go in my pocketbook to search for change. As I was looking through my Bible, shaking it out, a brand new ten dollar bill fell from the book. Right then I understood what the Bible meant in Exodus 1:12 when it said as they were afflicted they grew (NIV).

The Lord will allow problems to visit you frequently until you get to the point where you're determined to grow—to let it push you past what you're going through and realize He is God. The agitation is the revealer because it shows you how God can take your mess and transform it to a message, your test into a testimony and your hurt into helping someone. When the Lord makes what was once comfortable uncomfortable it is because He is trying to get you out of your comfort zone and into your greatest purpose zone. I've learned all things work together for the good even when it disturbs my will.

Realization is, "the act of becoming fully aware of something as a fact; the fulfillment or achievement of something desired or anticipated" (Google, 2016). There is more to life than just living. At some point on our roads to our destinies, we receive a rude awakening like the Apostle Paul. Act 9 tells us that while Paul was traveling on the road to Damascus, "suddenly a light from heaven flashed around him. He fell to the ground, and heard a voice say to him, "Saul, Saul why do you persecute me"?... "I am Jesus who you are persecuting" (vv. 3-6, NIV). When I take a look at the word "persecute", its synonyms are "oppress", "abuse", "mistreat" and "torture". At the time, Saul thought he was doing the right thing, but soon realized his life was going in the wrong direction. Maybe we are not murdering others as Saul did, but we can be guilty of a life of self-sabotage. When you begin to let God's plans unfold in your life, you begin to see things clearly and realize there is better waiting for you. It's time you realize God has a better plan for you.

Eleven years ago I found myself in a mess. Because I never dealt with the things in my childhood, I continuously looked for love in all the wrong people and things. This was the worst season of my life overall. I wanted to get out, but I didn't have the strength to leave because even though it was the wrong thing to do, I felt accepted on all levels. One day I was home and I heard a voice say to me, "Choose this day who you will serve. You can choose the blessings and the curse". It was that moment that I understood the choices I made had nothing to do with the will of God. It was at that moment that I understood that I had abused and mistreated myself based upon my desires and not God's. In that moment, I realized I could do all things through Christ Jesus (Philippians 4:13) and that I was the head and not the tail, above and not beneath, the lender and not the borrower (Deuteronomy 28:12-13). It was then that I realized that

I was an overcomer (Romans 8:37), and He that begun a good work in me shall be able to perform it to the day of Jesus Christ (Philippians 1:6).

Manifestations are, "an event, action, or object that clearly shows or embodies something, especially a theory or an abstract idea" (Google, 2016). Although I may not have arrived at my final destination, I can truly say after going through what I have experienced, God has truly showed me that if I just push through everything and recognize my worth in the process, then nothing will ever stop me from being my best me. It takes too much to play the part of someone else. So today I manifest in my life exactly what God wants because I'm no longer me, I'm me in HIM.

I challenge you today to find yourself. Learn who God is calling you to be. Pull yourself out of the depths from which you have been hiding yourself and be free to be you. You will not regret it. Look through each of the actions that had to happen for me to find myself and understand how you experienced those same things throughout your life. If you are stuck at a certain action, pray it through until He releases you to move forward. Being who you are in Christ is the best you that you can be. Manifest that person today.

Knowing Who You Are

Sophia Shamburger

Knowing Who You Are

Sophia Shamburger

As a child I was often asked, "Do you know who you are?" My reply was, "Yes, of course. I am a girl and my name is Cocoa". Cocoa was a nickname! I never used my given name.

Many of us go through life with a nickname that can sometimes make us forget how important our birth name is. We miss out on the value and great impact our given name holds. We go through life not realizing how much power we have within us—the very thing that GOD has designed us to be filled with: the anointing that lives deep within us all. From the beginning of time, the Creator ordained us to be more then conquerors. But for the anointing to be manifest from the inside out, we must come to a place in our lives where we make the choice to surrender to God the father and our Lord and Savior Jesus Christ.

Life has its ups and downs, but through it all we learn valuable lessons. For instance, think about childhood experiences in which you met people, developed relationships and felt the emotions that came along with success, trials, poor decision and lack of trust. Think about the times you had to work through issues with self-confidence, low self-esteem, lack of gratitude, the weakness of your spiritual walk and peer pressure to hide behind a mask pretending to be someone you weren't (or aren't if you still struggle with this today). All this led up to the emotional issues that became overbearing, unshakable and sometimes appeared immovable from your total being. As a child of God, you can walk in authority with power from the Holy Ghost. However, if you are like most of us, when challenges come your way you forget who you are and how much power is instilled in you from the Father.

We all were born into a world of good and evil, which makes us subject to many things that can make us fall short with God. As we grow, we see and learn from our parents, siblings, school teachers, peers, other extended family members, etc. With all that we learn, whether it's good or bad, we take it all in as we develop into teenagers who still don't understand what is happening around us or who we truly are within. Before we know it, here comes adulthood and most of us are more messed up than ever.

Some of us have been raised up in the church, while others of us have not experienced what it is like to be prayed for and loved unconditionally. We deal with so many issues that cause us to stumble and fall, taking away from us the realization of who we are and what we were created for. Many of us have experienced obstacles that brought great challenges, that showed our strength and weakness, and that led to even more difficult choices than those we have already made. We have begun to doubt that we will ever truly know who we are.

As we go through life living with bitterness, rejection and regrets, we wonder, "Where do we go from here?" You may ask yourself this question often. I have an answer for you, but you must get to the place where you realize that without God you will never be who you were created to be. God knows everything about us and is the only one who can show us who we really are. It's time to surrender it all unto the Lord thy God.

Take a moment of self-reflection, which will help lead you to your calling of destiny. God has a plan for us all. It is so important you understand this. Knowing God has a plan for your life is very important when things happen that are out of your control. I know it can be very discouraging. It's easy to become frustrated, to feel afraid and to question what the future holds. But when you have God, you can rest assured that He has it all under control and will not let you down. You will still experience trials but you will be comforted as the waves crash around you because you are standing firm upon the solid rock.

Putting your faith in God's plan allows you to trust that the events in your life are meant to be. It helps you to make the choices that must be made and realize things are not really out of control – they are under his control. There is a peace that can be found knowing that His plan is playing out in your life. When things are confusing for you, remember that God is in control and He loves you. Trust Him and His plans.

We all have a need for acceptance. In fact our self-concept is often determined by the approval or rejection of those around us. Whether we think about family, peers, business associates, fellow students or even Christian friends, we want to be loved and accepted by them or we feel the sting of rejection and start to question our value and worth. We tend to do and say what we hope will win people's favor. This tendency often carries over into our relationship with God. We feel we must somehow earn God's acceptance of us, so we end up acting out of a sense of guilt.

In the book of Romans, Paul expounds the doctrine of justification, the biblical foundation upon which a right relationship is built with ourselves, with others and with God. It frees us to be all that God intends for us (Romans 3:9-26). Open your eyes to the truth of your past and your future, then you can start to see manifestation of the miracles of God's purpose for your life.

To do this, try these two exercises: Awaking and Satisfaction:

"A Manifestation Now Moment" - Awakening Exercise: There is a time when it is essential to awaken to your purpose in life. That time is now. Even with our eyes open, we sometimes go through our days as if we're sleepwalking. These are the only days we have; we need to be aware of them. Say to yourself each morning, "I will be awake, really awake, today and forever more as I trust in Lord." Then commit to being fully present in each moment you experience today. Put down the cell phone for a bit, step away from the computer, be present in your life and fully aware of what the Lord is doing in and around you.

"A Manifestation Now Moment" - Satisfaction Exercise: We always want more—more possessions, money, popularity. Whatever it may be that we feel that we just don't have enough of, we try to find it or achieve it. Today become satisfied with the things that you already have and then sit back and watch God move on your behalf. Take a few minutes to write down three things every day that you are thankful for in your life. It does not matter how small or large they are, be sure to be thankful and watch how more comes into your life because you are good with what you already have.

Friends, whatever your season in life, it is never too late to understand who you are in Christ. You have been designed with a special purpose, passion and dream. Do not settle for what other people have told you that you will receive or become. Instead, reflect and search God's heart. Only He knows why He designed you and what he created you to become. Go straight to Him and stop asking others to define you. Only in God can you become all you were created to be. Grab hold of that truth today and soar high!

Your Purpose through Trials

Brianna Abdallahi

Your Purpose through Trials

Brianna Abdallahi

It can be hard to trust that you have a purpose when you are experiencing multiple and hard trials. They become blinders that block God's divine hand. Sometimes our situations can be so massive that we feel we have lost our purpose. I'd like to share some helpful scriptures to remind you that no matter what trials come, God will continually have a purpose for our lives. He created you and He will see you through each trial if you cry out to Him (1 Corinthians 10:13, NIV).

Secret Plan of God
- Ephesians 3
    - God saw to it that you were equipped, but you can be sure that it had nothing to do with your natural abilities. God can do anything, far more than you could ever imagine, guess, or request in your wildest dreams.
- Proverbs 4
    - When you walk, your steps will not be hindered, when you run you will not stumble

Showing Up
- Genesis 24
    - Season of your preparation process.
    - Reason for where you are at.
- God has given us the power to decree and declare things we need moved, shifted, and increased. Our mouth is the gateway of us

seeing things get done. When we open our mouth and speak to that mountain (trials in our life) we will begin to see things happen.

Treasure in Jars of Clay

- 2 Corinthians 4
    - o We have hidden treasures in jars of clay. Allow God to mold you into a masterpiece of art. You are His cherished treasure.

Race of Faith

- Hebrews 12
    - o Christian life parallel to a long distance race.
    - o You cannot run the race of life unless you lay aside any impediment that hinders you from putting forward your best effort.
- A distance race requires:
    - o Endurance
    - o Persistence
    - o Effort

True Beauty

- 1 Samuel 16:17
    - o Having the Holy Spirit within empowers a woman with vitality (life) and enthusiasm making her magnet (attract) to other people.
- A Christian woman's appearance should be a compliment to her inner spirit.
- Don't be discouraged or shaken when people talk about how you look on the outside.

- God did not choose you because of your looks, but God chose you because of your purpose that was predestined for your life.

Patience
- James 1
  - Potential a Christian woman has for maturity relates to the realization of her God-given destiny.
- You are striving to reach a goal that only God can enable you to achieve.

Nothing Too Hard For God
- Genesis 18
  - Yield yourself, so God can get the Glory out of your life.
- Position yourself in God.
- Press in.
- When you begin to move on God's behalf, He will move on yours.

Spiritual Gifts
- Ephesians 4
  - The Lord urgently wants you to walk worthy of the calling that you were called in. Having the absence of pride and bearing one another in Love. He gave these gifts for the equipping of His people to edify the body of Christ.

Receiving Your Calling

- Genesis 37
    - Joseph had dreams where God revealed His divine plan and purpose for Joseph. His brothers envied Joseph to the point where they wanted to kill him. Instead the brothers decided to sell Joseph to the Ishmaelites for 20 shekels and they took him to Egypt.
    - Joseph's dreams placed him in the line of those chosen by God to receive blessings.

Evidence of Personal Calling

- We have the confidence that we will hear His voice. We hear from Him because we have a personal relationship with God.
- Your personal calling is an opportunity to influence others.
- If we are God's children, His spirit will lead us.
- He can speak to us through His word, Holy Spirit, and prayers.
- The closer we walk with God the more we understand our part in His plan for the world.
- What are you most passionate about doing?
- What gifts and talents has God given you to equip you for what you're doing?

When We Are Tested Our Faith Is Also Tested

- James 1:2-8
    - Know that the testing of your faith produces patience.
- The potential a Christian woman has for maturity relates to the realization of her God-given destiny. She is striving to reach a goal that only God can enable her to achieve.

- If you feel you may lack such things as wisdom, joy, peace and confidence ask of God who will give you what you may lack liberally without question.
- When you ask God for anything, ask with confidence/faith that the God you serve will do it.

Fatal Distractions
- Satan is not after you, but after your destination.
- Iron sharpens Iron.
- Be around people who are like minded people.
- Intimacy is the Devil's biggest tool for distraction.
- Sometimes we don't know something is a distraction until it is too late.

Take Heed to God's Instruction
- Proverbs 4
  - If we take heed to God's instruction when we walk in His divine steps we will not hinder, create difficulties for someone or something, resulting in delay or obstruction.
- When we run, we will not trip or fall (Isaiah 40:31).
- Keep God's wisdom in your mind, emotions, and heart. His wisdom is your life.

HEADED FOR DESTRUCTION POEM

How do you stop something you didn't mean to start?
When did it become second nature for me to do what I please?
I'm in this circle for my own mess, trying to get out
Where's the exit sign?
I was doing so well
I had everything under control, but I looked the other way for 2 seconds
That quickly I was headed for destruction
I pray to God please take the taste out my mouth
The taste is too rich to let go
Every day I weigh myself down with my own sin
How do I stop this High that I am on?
I asked for forgiveness Again, Again, and Again
This time I can't ask
Why should I ask?
The guilt that I carry is too great for me to walk around with.
The knot in my stomach
Knowing I am wrong is too much for me to carry.
I crawl my way to your feet Again
I find you
You console me in my tears, Again
You tell me you love me, Again
You comfort me, Again
This time around I have to do better, I just have to
Even though this is my 5th time, I just have to
I refuse to continue on this road to destruction
No more self-destructing yourself.
Lord show me my next steps
Help me focus on you
Allow me to understand your will for me.

TESTIMONY

I am 21 years old and in my Junior year in college pursuing a degree in Mass Communications. People knew who I was because of the leadership role I held as the President of the Student Ambassadors Club. I represented not only Christ but the entire student body. People my age and older looked up to me everywhere I went. When you know God is with you, other people can see that too—even people who are not for you. I wrote this piece because I had to remind myself that I still have a beautiful purpose despite finding out that I am pregnant.

I was devastated at first. My first thought was to get an abortion because I wanted to cover up my sin; however, regardless of how I tried, God would not let it be. I was depressed, ashamed, and embarrassed to even pray. I just knew God was disgusted with me, but truthfully that was not the case. He reminded me that "All things work for our good" (Romans 8:28, NIV) and "No one knows the thoughts of God" (1 Corinthians 2:11).

I had to remember that His will is perfect even when it does not make sense to me. We cannot fathom the mind of God and His purpose. I still have a divine purpose even with this miracle in my womb. I am not perfect, but I am real. I cannot be ashamed of my trials even if they are self-inflicted because God will get the glory out of my life.

I realize people are going to talk about me, look at me, discredit me, but God will work it all out to serve a higher purpose. I share this continued testimony for women who are in the same trial or feel useless. I am here as a witness that God is Alpha in all your trials. We are blessed and highly favored by God.

Do not give up. Let the Lord do His perfect work. No matter how difficult it gets, your chapter is still being written. Surrender to the Lord, repent of your sins, and watch what God can do. The Bible assures us that "The Lord is close to the brokenhearted and saves those who are crushed in spirit" (Psalm 34:18). That means you too.

Why Me?

Nicole Bryant

Why Me?

Nicole Bryant

Have you ever said one of the following phrases in response to the trials and tribulations that you have walked or are walking through:

- "Enough is enough!"
- "Why me God?"
- "How much more can I take?"
- "I can't take no more!"?

I am here to offer hope if you answered, "Yes, I've said that many times in my life." So many times throughout my life I have asked those questions. Every time I asked, I heard Him say, "Why not you?" I remember thinking, "Really God? Why not me?" Then I would read Jeremiah 29:11 and understand exactly why I had to go through things, "For I know the thoughts that I think toward you, saith the Lord, thoughts of peace, and not of evil, to give you an expected end" (KJV).

Jeremiah 1:5 says, "Before I formed thee in the belly I knew thee; and before thou camest forth out of the womb I sanctified thee, and I ordained thee a prophet unto the nations" (KJV). From the first day I was born, the enemy has been in my midst. I was born early, at 8 months, in a hospital that did not have an incubator. As such, I had to be flown to a Manhattan hospital for further care until I was able to leave the hospital weeks later. Once I arrived home from the hospital, it was discovered that I was allergic to the formula and had to be rushed back to the hospital. The allergic reaction had turned me completely black and blue. On top of worrying about my early birth, you could imagine the horror of a mother having a baby with a terrible formula allergy. I thank God that "prayers of the righteous availeth much" (James 5:16, KJV). My grandmother, Isabel Lindsay, a woman of faith was able to move mountains. I fully believe it is because of her prayers that I survived every attack. Even the doctors had told my mother it was a miracle that I was alive.

Growing up in a single-parent home, there was not a lot of quality time due to the fact that my mother worked extremely hard to provide for her family. She was so overworked, traveling 2 1/2 hours each way just to support us. In my early education, my grades began to drop. Luckily, I came across some great teachers like Mrs. Bailey, Mrs. Britt and Mrs. Tate, who instilled positive values in me and pushed me to succeed. I was falling behind in my education due to battling depression, but they never lost hope in me.

I had such a hard time dealing with things that in junior high I was referred to see a counselor with my mother. In the middle of my high school days, my mother got married and relocated us to the Bronx. I now had to travel 2 hours back and forth to school. As a result of the move, I became rebellious and very laid back. I began to slack in my school work again. In my junior year of high school, my grades fell tremendously but I was still able to maintain a high State test score. The Board of Education had a plan to help keep me on track and put me in a program called College Now. I was able to go to Kingsboro College while still attending high school. It was nothing but the favor of God. As a result, I graduated high school on time with a partial scholarship for college! I chose to attend BMCC. I also began to work in the Fashion Industry, which was my passion. I later made the decision to relocate back to Brooklyn with my Aunt Claudia. At that time my scholarship ended, there no extra money to continue college. My mother always taught me the value of working hard and the importance of keeping a job, which was a task in the Fashion Industry because companies opened and closed often. I was able to find a new job to get back on track and start a new me.

Months later, I came to find out that I was expecting my first child. One day, on my way to Christmas shopping on the train to Yonkers with my sister Lakeisha, I started to miscarry on the train. At the time I was only 5 1/2 months pregnant. We redirected back to Brooklyn and I began to lose feeling in my legs once we got off the train. Anxiety set in and I began to hysterically panic. With no help from the token booth clerk, a homeless man came to my rescue. I truly believe that angels come in all forms. He had assisted me until the ambulance arrived.

Dealing with the loss of my child, I was then informed that I had cancer and had to undergo chemo. I thought to myself, "God this has got to be a mistake. How much can I take at once? Really God? Why me?" I had gathered some strength to go back to work and started my chemo treatments. Living with family members, some issues arose and I decided to get an apartment with a high school friend. This friendship did not work out and it ended with me becoming homeless. At first I stayed in a house that rented rooms, but it was so unclean and I was not used to that life so I decided to leave. Being a private person, I didn't want to express my hardships to others so I slept at my job while my coworkers were away at the California office for Fashion week. Not being able to continue to stay at my job, I then resorted to staying at friends' houses. This had become very overwhelming. My faith began to waver but I thank God for my best friend for more than 30 years now, Kimmy Gayle, because she encouraged me at the time that things would get better.

Why Me?

In this time of need, Carolyn Sanders opened her doors to me to have a stable place to live. Working to get my own place, once again I lost my job. This time I wanted to pursue Cosmetology School. This required a cosigner to start school but couldn't find one in the allotted time. Just when I thought things were about to get better, stumbling blocks stood in my way. Once again, God had an angel in the midst: Ms. Sondra McClarin, who spoke to the owner, Mr. T, and God touched his heart. We worked out a way for me to pay for school. With extraordinary teachers, Ms. Sondra and Ms. Cheryl helped me to complete Cosmetology school even with my hardships.

After completing school, I worked for Geraldine Haynes in Gerri's Place Salon in Brooklyn, NY where I felt complete again, doing what I loved to do. I happily worked there for six years. Once again the dark cloud came and business slowed down due to the economy. I made the decision to leave and return to Corporate America in the Fashion industry.

Now that the rain was gone, or so I thought, my sister Lakeisha was killed. That was like a piece of my world ending. We were like Siamese twins; when you saw her, you saw me. Even through my homelessness, she was always right there. Through that rough path, Lakeisha had relocated first to Connecticut and then North Carolina, where she was killed from senseless gun violence. To replace a part of me that was lost, my boyfriend at the time proposed to me and we were married the following year on her birthday.

It wasn't long after that a whirlwind came to destroy my life again. Everything hit me at once; with a failing marriage and depression setting in. I lost thirty pounds in three weeks, which caused my doctor to prescribe me anti-depressants and acid reflux medication. He even prescribed me needles, which I had to administer myself, for my reoccurring migraines. With the fear of needles and sickness from the other medications, I discontinued all of the medication on my own and decided to trust God for my complete healing: past and current.

Some things only come through fasting and praying. Through all of my struggles, God had put people by my side to help me get through it. My First Lady, Drusilla White; Prophetess France Gray and Minister Gem Oxley, and now Evangelist Antoinette Ates; were the support team we all need in our lives. They helped me build a true relationship with the Lord. In the midst of obstacles in my marriage, I found out I had a hernia so bad the doctor said he had not seen one that bad in 26 years of practicing. The surgery to repair it took more than two hours. When it was over, he told me he didn't know how I was alive. He knew that it was the work of God.

With my support team teaching me the real purpose of fasting and praying, God had answered my prayers with a prophecy from First Lady Sabrina Shaw, which caused chains that were holding me to break! I was set free. I knew for sure that God loved me and had purpose for my life. I began to see life differently and now I was set free from the spirit of bondage. The dark clouds became sunshine.

During this transition, my mother-in-law, Sarah Bryant, became sick with stomach cancer. I assisted in taking care of her until her passing in 2004. Two years later, we discovered that my mother's breast cancer came back. At the same time, my stepfather was fighting prostate cancer and dementia. With them living in South Carolina, this became very stressful for me. I felt like a present day Job. I went through a divorce but God gave me peace through the storm.

Working in the Accounting department in the Garment District had come to a halt as the company had to close its doors. I was directed back to my passion and got a new job at Hair Design Institute, which after nine years and counting, I am not only teaching Cosmetology but also helping my students find their purpose through their storms using my life experiences to show them troubles don't last always. My stepfather passed away in August 2011, then my mom followed right behind him in October. My mom fought a good fight to the very end. She was a nurse for more than 20 years in Calvary Hospital in Bronx, NY. After relocating to South Carolina she became a spokeswoman for Relay for Life, a cancer organization, while dealing with the illness herself. The disease was the very thing that was ended her life. Romans 8:28 says, "All things work together for the Good of them that Loves the Lord and is called according to His Purpose" (KJV). My mom's purpose was fulfilled. My support team grew with addition of Elder Vernise Couch, my Aunts Lynda Lindsay and Victoria Bryant, who were a great help at this time with the transitioning and then the passing of my mother.

I see God working daily as I continue to seek Him for the things that He has ordained for my life and not the things I thought I wanted. Now knowing that God had a plan for all these downfalls, I see and fulfill my purpose with expectation for greater things. With my sister Simone Thomas holding me accountable to the things of God on day-to-day basis, I will continue to walk in the will of God all the days of my life. I am a licensed Cosmetologist and licensed Cosmetology Instructor, through which I mentor and encourage women and young girls on a daily basis about how to keep pressing until their changes come. My family, friends, personal customers, and students look to me for guidance in situations in their personal lives. I am glad that my trials and tribulations qualify me to assist them to see their true value in life. I have opened my doors to people who needed a place to stay because somebody opened their doors for me and I know how it feels to be homeless. I counsel women in broken and distressed relationships, and even failed marriages, back to wholeness. I go out and speak to young ladies as a motivational speaker to let them know our trials help us see what we are made of and it helps us to fulfill our purpose. At work, I help students find employment to help with the necessities of life.

Not everything we go through in life is good. Even a farmer has to put his seeds into soil fertilized with manure to get a great harvest. Therefore when you feel overwhelmed, just know you are an overcomer. The times in which you feel you failed, let your faith fail you not. Even when it seems like you are the walking dead, trust that there is a more abundant life. When you feel you are the victim, you are really victorious. So if you asked, prayed or even questioned, "Why Me Lord?" just know that asking that may symbolize "will have you mentor effectively" because everything we go through in life is to help someone else. It states in Job 23:10, "But He knoweth the way that I take: when he hath tried me, I shall come out as pure gold" (KJV). Therefore, after being tried by the fire you will come out shining as pure gold if you don't give up. By persevering, after trials tribulations purpose will be fulfilled. So next time you are wondering, "Why me?" stop and take time to praise God that you are about to go to new heights!

Their Thanks

For every story we have, there are people who made it possible. This is the opportunity to read the thanks the ladies have prepared for those who made this book possible.

"I will give thanks to you, LORD, will all my heart;
I will tell of your wonderful deeds."
~Psalm 9:1

Charlotte Ellis Colbert

I thank God for everything He has allowed me to experience in my life that has prepared me for this moment in time.

I would like to express my deepest appreciation and thanks to my wonderful parents, Earnest Ellis Jr. & Gladys Marie Ellis. Thank you for your constant support, encouragement, unconditional love, and most of all for teaching me how to pray! I love you!

A special thanks to my brother, Napoleon Ellis. You have never who has never left my side, even when living miles apart! Also a super special to my niece, Kayla Ellis. You were there when I needed you most. I love you both!

A heart-filled thanks and appreciation to my friend, Bridget Davis, and her entire family: James, Jamie and Jireh. Bridget, thanks for your constant words of encouragement, relentless prayer, challenging me to reach higher, lending a listening ear on countless occasions, and your genuine desire for me to "WIN". Your acts of sisterly love will never be forgotten!

Thank you Mrs. Brenda Postell and Ms. Shirley Crum for your unconditional love and encouragement throughout my life. You have exemplified women of faith, courage, and strength.

I would like to thank my entire Simmons and Ellis family. Particular thanks to my Aunt, Catherine Simmons Thomas, Cendra Simmons and Authenia Ellis: Thank you for always wanting the best for me, the countless hours of talk time, always being available and loving me unconditionally.

To my friends, Iris Young Clarke, Co-Sandra Roche, LaShun Jenkins, Sherri King, Kandis Singleton Patrick, and Lori Scott (and sending thanks to Heaven for my dear friend Trisha Sherfield Polite): Thank you for all of the times we have spent that have brought me to this very important time of my life. I would not be the person I am today without each experience we have shared.

To my Humana Team - TMT 30: Thank you for always encouraging me and pushing me to step into the water without hesitation. Nkosi Gilmore, thank you for being a leader who allowed us to remain balanced. A special thanks to Shay Bussey, Bershaya Eason, Lashawn Bagley and Mosheika Brown, Kayte Larsen, and Christie Baldwin.

Dr. Renee Sunday: Thank you from the bottom of my heart. Your guidance, inclusion, prayers and invitation to be a part of this opportunity will never be forgotten. Thanks for always remaining humble and offering a light of hope for all. You are dynamic in every sense of the word and I pray that God continues to bless you!

To my children, Dwan Colbert, Jr. (DJ); Taylor Colbert; and Jaden Colbert: None of this would be possible without your support and encouragement. You guys have offered your love and support in so many different ways and I am forever grateful that God chose me to be your mom. When our family dynamics took on a new face, you remained balanced and filled every gap. Words will not express how much I love you and appreciate You! You will forever be my dynamic kids!

Thank you to Heaven on Earth Ministry, Prophet Daniel Powell and Prophetess Esther Powell & Jerusalem Church of God By Faith: Your spiritual guidance helped me through some challenging times.

For those I could not name, I love and thank each and every one of you! "Manifest Now!"

Trina Hardy

God, Thank you.

I humbly acknowledge the many people who have impacted my life throughout the years and have been very influential to me in tremendous ways.

Special thanks to Renee Sunday for giving me this opportunity.

Thank to Kabiru Razaq for his godly input in helping to polish up my story.

Thanks to Bishop Matthew Odum, Sr.; Elder Antwain Turner; my parents, Carolyn & Joseph Hardy; my siblings; my daughter, Trinity; my friends; family and church family.

And finally, to you the reader: Thank you for your support. May the contents of this book be a blessing to you.

Renee Sunday

I thank God for His love, grace, and mercy. With much prayer and seeking God as to the direction and message to take this project, I truly gained clarity of the support of my family. Gratitude to my parents, Mr. William and Rosetta Sunday, for being the foundation of putting God first, loving, grateful, a cheerful giver and my earthly angels as parents.

My sister and brother-in-law, Cassandra and Clifford Williams: Thank you for being my role models of the spirit of excellence in everything you do and say.

My beloved aunts, uncles, nieces, and nephews: Thank you for your love and igniting the passion to walk in my destiny.

To my inner circle: Thank you for praying, pushing and being pivotal points in my life. Your love and support is divine and heartfelt.

To my fellow co- authors: I thank God for your predestined path that included me. Your passion for your fellow man to have manifestations now is expressed in your daily walk in your purpose.

To the readers: You have a calling, purpose and destiny. Your gifts are already inside of you. The world is awaiting your dreams, goals, and purpose to blossom and flourish to all people. Blessings.

Remember: Manifestations Now!!!! Believe, Trust, Walk Out Your Destiny.

Jamila Monroe

First and foremost, I would like to thank my heavenly Father for all He has done and is doing for me. Thank you for rescuing me.

Thanks to my children, who I call my "Five Heartbeats", I thank God for each one of you.

Thank you to my mom. Where would I be if it wasn't for your dedication?

To my siblings: Love you all.

To Dr. Kishma George: Thank you for believing in me and opening doors.

To Dr. Renee Sunday for the opportunity to be a part of this wonderful journey.

And last but never least, thanks to my KCWC family. I truly pastor the best set of people.

Sophia Shamburger

I first want to give all thanks and honor to my Lord and Savior.

Thank you to my amazing, beautiful mother, Majesty Eleanor Shamburger; my sister, Duchess Annette Armstrong Lester; my brother, the Duke John H. Shamburger, Jr.; and my children, who are the loves of my life and my greatest blessings: Prince Tyrone Peterson II, Princess Germanek C. Peterson, Prince Marquice N. Pierce, Princess Erika M. Swain, Princess Akira E. Swain, and the Genius Prince Eric N. Swain II (aka Dynamite "E"). I love you all and appreciate all of your love and support.

Thank you Dr. Renee Sunday for seeing something in me and supporting me and having faith in me.

Thank you Pastor Willie E. Robertson of the Mount Pleasant Baptist Church of Twin Oaks, PA for your continued support, stretching, love, and grace. I value and honor you and am thankful to serve under you.

Brianna Abdallahi

God, I thank you for the vision and the confidence to take the first step in writing my chapter. You have been with me every step of the way. You never gave up on me, even when I gave up on myself.

Mom and Dad, I thank you for always encouraging me to do what I am passionate about.

Nina Thomas, I thank you for being my biggest fan even when I didn't believe in myself. You always gave me a boost of confidence.

To my unborn child, even though you were unexpected, I believe God has purpose for your life. You are such a beautiful gift. I love you with all my heart. This is just the beginning of a new chapter for the both of us.

Nicole Bryant

I would first and foremost, like to thank God who is the head of my life and without Him none of this would be possible. To my Grandmother, who is that matriarch of the Lindsay family, may she rest in peace. To my Mother, Alma Lindsay-Bristow, who instilled in me faith, love, and prayer which caused me to be the strong woman who I am today: though gone you will never be forgotten because you'll always be in my heart. To my biological family, thank you from the bottom of my heart for all the love and guidance that you have shown and given me continuously throughout my life.

To my Bishop Jeffrey White and First Lady Drusilla White, God could not have given me better Spiritual Parents. To all my godchildren, I love you guys dearly. My church family, God couldn't have put me in the midst of a better Spiritual Brothers and Sisters. To my friends, many thanks for showing yourselves friendly and keeping me accountable for God's purpose in my life. To my prayer partners, far and near, your prayers kept me standing in the midst of the fire and we know prayers of the righteous availeth much.

To Apostle Patricia Wiley and Bishop Zebedee Dowtin, thank you for prophetically speaking this book into my life. To Kishma George, thank you for helping me to fulfill the plan of God with referring me to be a part of this book project; I am so ever thankful. To all the women and young ladies who God has called me to touch in one way or another, thank you for allowing me to be an inspiration, mentor and motivator in your life.

The Foundation

The Sunday Foundation - A foundation of Action

Propelling individuals into their purpose in life. SF creates, finds and supports individuals who want to improve their thinking, wellbeing and offer opportunities that will empower individuals to obtain a fulfilled, joyful and thriving life.

The Sunday Foundation

The Founder

The Sunday Foundation (SF) is a 501(c)3 nonprofit organization. SF is a foundation of action. Propelling individuals into their purpose in life. SF creates, finds and supports individuals who want to improve their thinking and wellbeing, as well as who want to offer opportunities that will empower individuals to obtain a fulfilled, joyful and thriving life.

SF's Founder Dr. Renee Sunday, the visionary of the non profit The Sunday Foundation states: "I have practiced anesthesia for over thirteen years. My mission is to encourage and empower others to enjoy life, share their message and obtain their dreams. Furthermore, I enjoy being an instrument to render services to others and to show compassion, love, and the standard of care."

Besides being an Anesthesiologist Dr. Sunday is a radio and television personality – Host of Good Deeds Radio & TV Show, Platform Builder, Grief & Loss Specialist, Group Counselor, Motivational & Inspirational Coach, Passion & Purpose Guru, Author and Publisher.

Dr. Sunday experienced loss of both her brother William Sunday, Jr. and Godson - Eyianlijah. During time at the hospitals, especially while in the intensive care unit (ICU), she noticed supportive families were tired and physically exhausted. Many of the families were in need of basic necessities and support for themselves.

Sunday Foundation (SF) was birthed to be a part of the solution to satisfy the needs of families. There are several existing organizations that help in this task as well. SF fervently will join the purpose to remedy the lack of others and continue to be one of the extended family members of one family at a time.

Our Mission

Our Mission is Serving Individuals to embark and obtain their purpose throughout communities near and far. Opportunities are few and far between. SF is here to bridge the gap with programs, necessities, and resources to serve and tailor to meet the needs of each individual.

We will accomplish the mission through Programs, Seminars, Workshops, Awards and Recognition plus other benchmarked resources for individuals to advance and propel forward in life.

For more information go to: www.thesundayfoundation.org